I HAD THE CRAZIEST DREAM

In celebration of the Magic and Mystery of the Dreamtime

Victoria

Copyright © 2008 by Victoria Rabinowe
First Edition

Bright Shadow Press
VictoriaDreams@mac.com
www.VictoriaDreams.com
1432 Don Gaspar
Santa Fe, NM 87505 U.S.A.

ISBN 978-0-9819045-0-4

Library of Congress Cataloguing in Publication Data

Rabinowe, Victoria
    I had the craziest dream last night / twelve creative explorations into the genius of the night mind / by Victoria Rabinowe
    Cm.

ISBN 978-0-9819045-0-4
1. Dreams.   2. Creativity.   3. Self-Help.   4. Psychology.   5. Diaries.   6. Art-Techniques.
LCCN 2008905851

Graphic Design by Sean Wells
Twilight Design Studio | www.twilightstudio.com | design@twilightstudio.com
Edited by Freya Diamond, Alex Fischer, Jean Stratton
Illustrations and text by Victoria Rabinowe

All rights reserved. No part of this book may be used or reproduced in any form or by any electronic or mechanical means including photocopying, recording or by any information storage and retrieval systems without written permission except in the case of brief quotations in critical articles or reviews.

I HAD THE CRAZIEST DREAM LAST NIGHT

TWELVE CREATIVE EXPLORATIONS INTO THE GENIUS OF THE NIGHT MIND

Written and Illustrated by
VICTORIA RABINOWE

Graphic Design by Sean Wells

BRIGHT SHADOW PRESS

THE ADVENTURE IS ON

FOREWORD

You have done it now.
The adventure is on.
You have jumped the fence,
swung over the chasm,
entered the rapids,
clicked your ruby red slippers.

You've opened this book.
and this book will open you.

This book, this stunning graphic work, this vibrant coaching manual embodies philosophy and practices for entering your dreams. It is as profound and thoughtful as it is provocative, generously offering guidance and engaging creative exercises, a shared journey between you and the artist Victoria Rabinowe in I HAD THE CRAZIEST DREAM LAST NIGHT.

To live attuned to your dreams, to have creative and expressive means for honoring and following them, is to live an informed, imaginative, attentively curious, richly motivated dialogue with Self and with the World.

Dreams are the mythic stories of our lives, spun one thread at a time. Dreams carry the seeds of our gradually emerging future, the links to our ancestors, the whispers of the daily world and all its events.

Dreams defy the logic and the ego boundaries of the awake mind. They do not reveal their intent or intelligence easily; their treasure is offered through respectful listening and inquisitive creativity. As with all relationships, communication with one's own dreams is dependent on specialized, sensitive skills, best learned from an active, articulate, generous practitioner.

You are in the company of an extraordinary artist and dreamer. Victoria Rabinowe lives what she writes and draws what she dreams. Each project offered here has evolved through concentrated, highly personal dream work, and through more than a decade's focused, creatively innovative work in her Art of the Dream *group settings.*

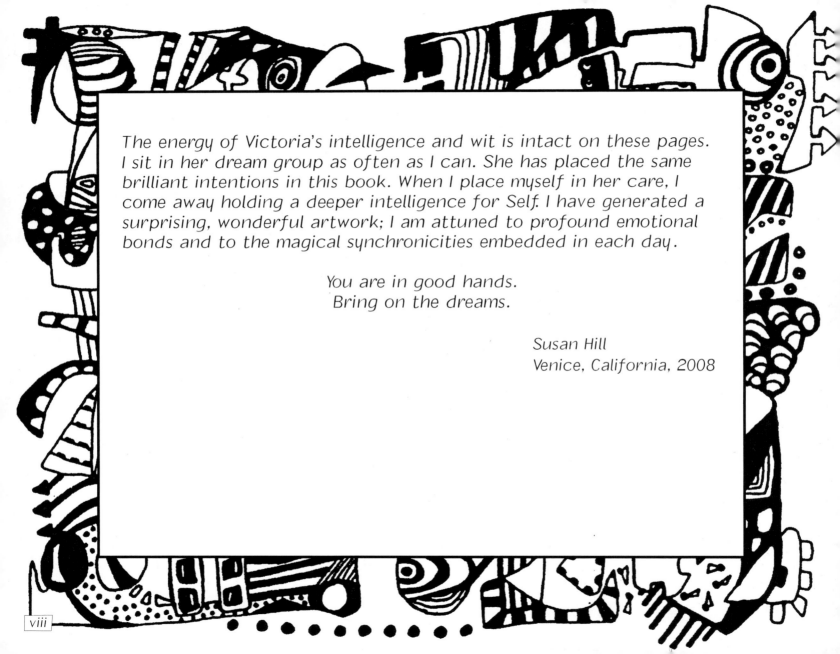

The energy of Victoria's intelligence and wit is intact on these pages. I sit in her dream group as often as I can. She has placed the same brilliant intentions in this book. When I place myself in her care, I come away holding a deeper intelligence for Self. I have generated a surprising, wonderful artwork; I am attuned to profound emotional bonds and to the magical synchronicities embedded in each day.

> You are in good hands.
> Bring on the dreams.

Susan Hill
Venice, California, 2008

x

TABLE OF CONTENTS

THE ADVENTURE IS ON ~ foreword vi
ACKNOWLEDGEMENTS xii
ART OF THE DREAM ~ preface xiv
MESSAGES FROM THE MUSE ~ introduction xviii
CHAOS INTO CREATIVITY xx
STORIES OF THE NIGHT ~ recording your dreams xxii
TRACES OF THE JOURNEY xxiii
STANDING AT THE THRESHOLD xxv

1. THE DREAM SCRIBE — 26
2. LEXICOGRAPHER ~ symbol maker — 38
3. ENIGMA ~ beyond question — 58
4. THE POLYMORPHIC SELF ~ the inner eye — 68
5. CARTOGRAPHER ~ mapping the dreamscape — 82
6. SYNCHRONICITY — 92
7. POUR YOUR HEART OUT — 104
8. ME AND MY SHADOW — 114
9. REMEMBRANCE OF THINGS PAST ~ the inner monologue — 126
10. THE POISON PEN ~ confronting the inner bully — 136
11. KEEPER OF THE ARCHIVES ~ little altars everywhere — 146
12. AMAZING GRACE — 156

THE DREAM TEAM 166
ETHICS STATEMENT 181

ACKNOWLEDGEMENTS

Thank you to all those who inspired me and believed in me.

Stephen Aizenstat, Emil Altman, Diana Adair, William Corbett, Eric Craig, Tom Crockett, Gina D'Ambrosio, Lisle Drake, Rita Dwyer, Heath Frost, Sally Hill, Victoria Hughes, Ruth Lantz, Alicia Lauritzen, Katherine Leiner, Laurie Leitch, Janet Lowe, Chrystal Oppenheimer, Mary Pat Mann, Jill Markus, Barbara Murphy, Nancy Paap, Miriam Randall, Gail Rieke, Joanne Rochon, Eric Rothschild, Richard Russo, Genie Shenk, Alan Siegel, Linda St. Germain, Barbara Sunshine, Robert Van de Castle, Carol Warner, Daryl Wells, Cynthia West, Sandra Wright, Esperanza Zane.

ART OF THE DREAM

PREFACE

I love the language that spills onto my journal pages as I record my dreams. I am never so clever or inventive when I am awake! It has always been a struggle for me to write; yet in my study, I have volumes of wild, colorful, dramatic, shocking, zany, beautiful, foolish and poetic dream stories.

These narratives have become the raw material for my paintings, drawings, digital art, artists' books, assemblage, collage and fiber art. The blending of creative arts with dreams has allowed me to explore the mystery of my inner universe. Over the years, this body of work has created an astonishing self-portrait.

In 1992, I dreamt of sailing off to sea with a blind boatman for a captain. Shortly afterwards, in an act of faith, inspired in part by my dream, I sold my prosperous and nationally acclaimed Santa Fe gallery to embark on a search for an unknown destiny. During my sabbatical from worldly matters, I developed a daily practice of meditation using active imagination where I recorded and illustrated the journeys I took. Synchronistically, a conference of the International Association for the Study of Dreams was held in Santa Fe where I became inspired to include the musings, memories, narrative imagery and poetry of my dreams in my journals.

The dream work inspired me to develop weekly studio workshops based upon my passion for creative endeavors. My work led me to study advanced DreamTending at Pacifica Graduate Institute. To date, I have taught over five hundred workshops, seminars and retreats in the Art of the Dream for therapists, educators, spiritual guidance counselors, writers, artists and dreamers from all walks of life.

Early in the development of my Art of the Dream workshops, one of my students brought in a classic nightmare of being dismembered by a buzz saw. She was clearly shaken during the telling of the dream and frightened by the emotions it brought forth. During the class, she transformed the image of the bloody scene into a dynamic red metallic mobile followed by a dramatic re-scripting of the dream. By the end of the class laughter and tears had replaced

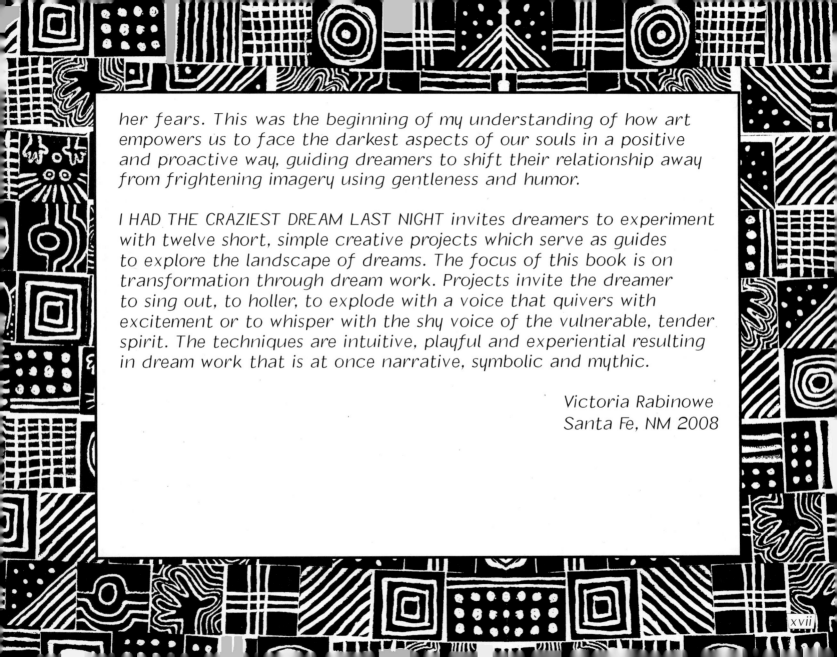

her fears. This was the beginning of my understanding of how art empowers us to face the darkest aspects of our souls in a positive and proactive way, guiding dreamers to shift their relationship away from frightening imagery using gentleness and humor.

I HAD THE CRAZIEST DREAM LAST NIGHT invites dreamers to experiment with twelve short, simple creative projects which serve as guides to explore the landscape of dreams. The focus of this book is on transformation through dream work. Projects invite the dreamer to sing out, to holler, to explode with a voice that quivers with excitement or to whisper with the shy voice of the vulnerable, tender spirit. The techniques are intuitive, playful and experiential resulting in dream work that is at once narrative, symbolic and mythic.

Victoria Rabinowe
Santa Fe, NM 2008

MESSAGES FROM THE MUSE

INTRODUCTION

Dreams come laden with metaphor and symbolism, yet many individuals complain that their dreams do not mean anything. They seem confusing, perplexing and peculiar. Yet, it is precisely this peculiarity that lures the curious dreamer on. Those of us who have fallen under the spell of our dreams have become enchanted by a world of mystery and paradox. Even when we have some conscious notion of what the meaning might be, our dreams have insights that are veiled in metamorphic transformations. A wellspring of inspiration opens. Dreams are filled with surprises!

Deeply mysterious and beyond our conscious understanding, dreams have no substance, yet are our close and constant companions. They mirror our inner vital energy. The animation, the action and the flow of the dream narrative provide a map of our individual life force. Our dreams are expansive enough to hold the complex stories of our lives. They explore the paths we have taken and the paths not taken.

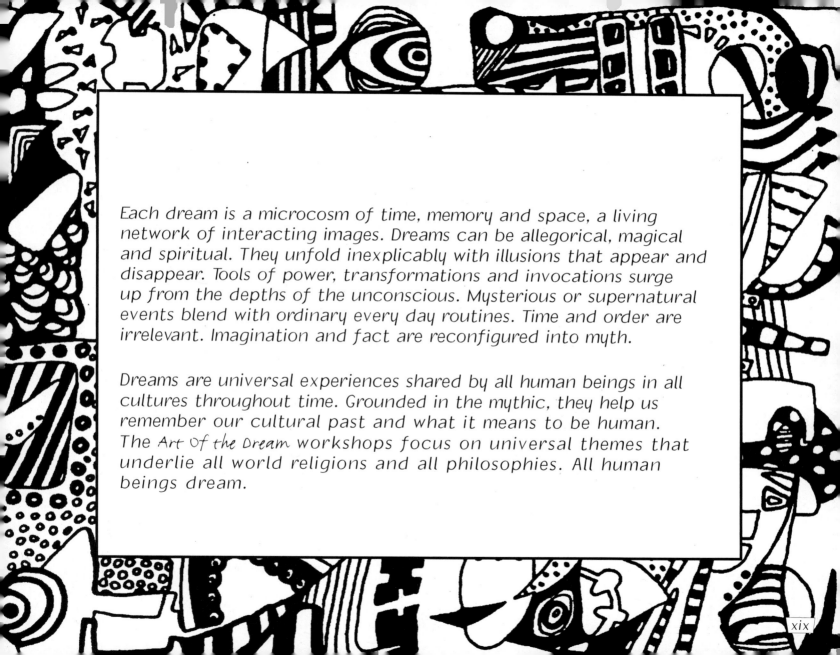

Each dream is a microcosm of time, memory and space, a living network of interacting images. Dreams can be allegorical, magical and spiritual. They unfold inexplicably with illusions that appear and disappear. Tools of power, transformations and invocations surge up from the depths of the unconscious. Mysterious or supernatural events blend with ordinary every day routines. Time and order are irrelevant. Imagination and fact are reconfigured into myth.

Dreams are universal experiences shared by all human beings in all cultures throughout time. Grounded in the mythic, they help us remember our cultural past and what it means to be human. The Art Of the Dream workshops focus on universal themes that underlie all world religions and all philosophies. All human beings dream.

CHAOS INTO CREATIVITY

Many of our dreams feel like a spin on the Wheel of Fortune. Our nocturnal narratives whirl about as if we were revolving disks in a relentlessly moving machine. We circumnavigate around an orbit of adventures where we spiral in and out of control. We travel around and around in circles with little result. We find ourselves striving and struggling without achieving anything but purposeless repetition. Recurring dream images haunt us. Repeating themes gnaw at us clamoring for our attention.

Dreams often come as perplexing or nightmarish narratives filled with unexpected dangers, toils and snares. Such a troubling dream is often more real than reality. The power of the dream world can hold us in its imaginal grip at the point of a knife, stirring us to our core and disrupting our innermost composure.

If we deny parts of ourselves that we do not want to acknowledge, hidden layers of protection become more complex with time. We all have a tendency to avoid feelings once the imagery gets too intense, *too disturbing or too painful. Unfortunately, some of the best parts of ourselves get hidden away as well. The dream provides a mirror image of this shadowy realm with all its treasures. We project the best and the worst of ourselves onto the images in our dreams.*

We become active dream workers when our feelings are overruled by the passionate search for our truth. No matter how perplexing or fearful, within each dream, there is a core of knowing that is always present.

STORIES OF THE NIGHT

RECORDING YOUR DREAMS

If you do not consider yourself a dreamer, start now. Keep a journal, a pen and a small light by the side of your bed. Ask for a dream before you go to sleep. Stay in bed for a few moments in the morning before getting up into the activity of the day. Train yourself to jot down any dream material or fragments whether they make sense or not. The more you work with dreams, the more you will be able to remember them. If time permits, write a log about the events and emotions from the day before. Then, according to your feelings about the dream, choose one or more of the twelve projects presented here to jump-start your journaling.

TRACES OF THE JOURNEY

If we open to the richness of our nightly narratives, our dreams become our muses, guardians of our emotions and the genius of our creativity. Dreams are the connection to our deepest, authentic creative source.

When a dream is looked upon in the light of day, it seems altered by space, time and shifting universes. At first we see only the distortions that push us away from reality. The two worlds of waking and sleeping seem to have little relationship to one another. However, when the dreamer looks closely, there are recognizable patterns fused in an unpredictable series of relationships.

The dream is a mystery which the rational mind cannot solve. To be curious is at the core of being a dreamer. To make sense of a dream, we need to learn how to shift away from our usual strategies for finding answers. Because dreams are often strange and inexplicable, it can be helpful to access them through visual arts, creative writing, movement and drama. When we reenter the dream space through art, we are meeting the dream in its own language of metaphor and symbol.

STANDING AT THE THRESHOLD

Each project is designed so that you can journal for a short amount of time or elaborate when you have the opportunity. There is no need to follow the order of the chapters. You may choose to work through all the projects with one dream, or you may choose a particular project to suit a specific dream. If you love to draw, paint and sculpt, you can follow the themes and allow your dream to unfold on paper, canvas or clay. If you love theater, you can use the projects to create monologues and performance pieces. Feel free to mix and match. You will find a fresh and creative exploration somewhere in these pages.

Begin in the place of Not Knowing. *You do not need to have any idea where you are going or what the meaning of the dream images may be. Trust the evocative projects to move your dream work forward. Listen to your heart and let go of the interference of your mind.*

To imagine means to 'image forth'
to give shape & context to things
we would otherwise find inexplicable.

Carl Gustav Jung

THE DREAM SCRIBE

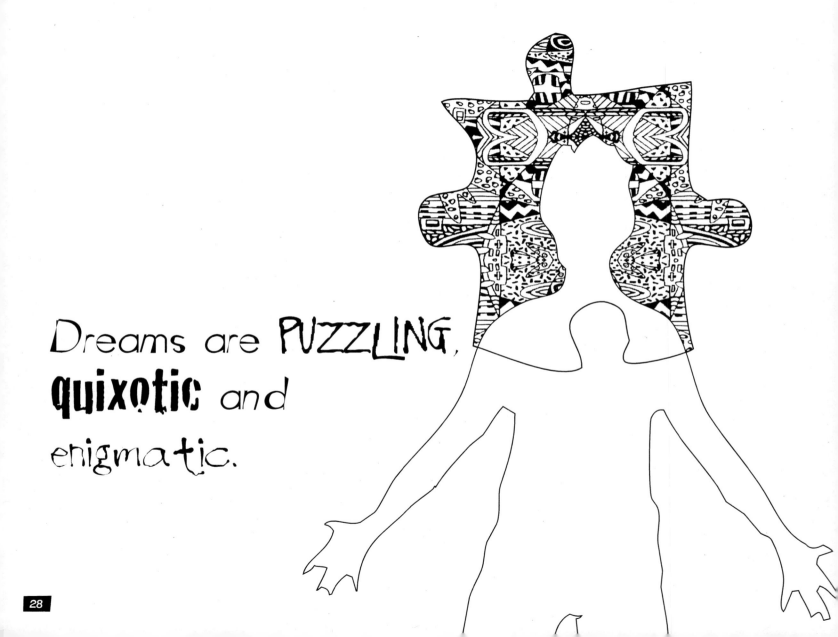

Dreams are PUZZLING, **quixotic** and enigmatic.

Before shaping an understanding
of the dream,
it is helpful to take inventory of
the **structural** elements.

TITLE

CREATE a title as if the dream were a story.

cred Songs Healing Herbs Double Headed Monkey Man Museum of Moons Daily Sanctity of Aurora Two
eashed Monster Annie Comes Home A Delicate Balance Drawn to the Sun Green Baby Gone Wild El
atloaf The Whole Tooth Rescuing Elephants This Side of Disaster Encroachin   The Pieces Fit Together Hazar
y Health Family Amulet Room Filled with Fishes A Helpless Man We   Out of Control Unrepen
pires Nursing the Unknown Babe A Big Gaping Wound Fligh   Dogs Bitter S
headed Blue Tin Shoes Colors of the Rainbow Reunion of Gian   t My
Car Dies a Perfect Fit Taking Flight Smeared with Paint He
rch Narrow Channel Split the Atom My House is Burning The
s Let the Red Bird Go The Cave's Nectar Our Black Roo
ut Elvis Gathering of Women Tarantula Bite I Won't Co
tamination Enormous Skunks Flying Naked Natur
union with Frogs Opportunity for Happiness Falls Shor
er Dies Sacred Songs Healing Herbs Double Headed
Fools Unleashed Monster Annie Comes Home A Deli
Elusive Meatloaf The Whole Tooth Rescuing Elepha
ether Hazardous to my Health Family Amulet Room
trol Unrepentant Vampires Nursing the Unknown B
gs Bitter Sands Beheaded Blue Tin Shoes Colors of
Eat My Arms My Car Dies a Perfect Fit Taking
st Subterranean Church Narrow Channel Split the
ce An Enchanting Mess Let the Red Bird Go The Cave's Nectar Our Black Root White Wash The Fourth Piece

STORY LINE

Write a brief summary of the dream using first person, present tense.

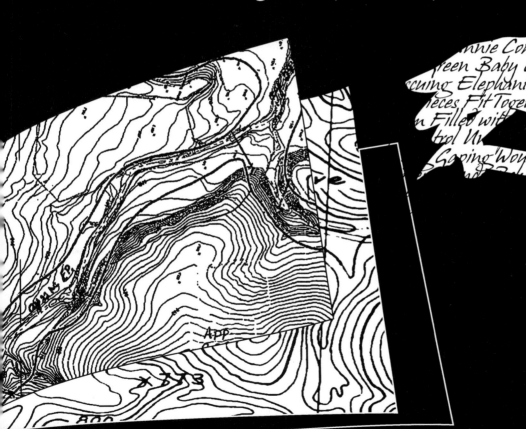

THEME

Is there a dominant motif, a common thread that RUNS THROUGH the dream?

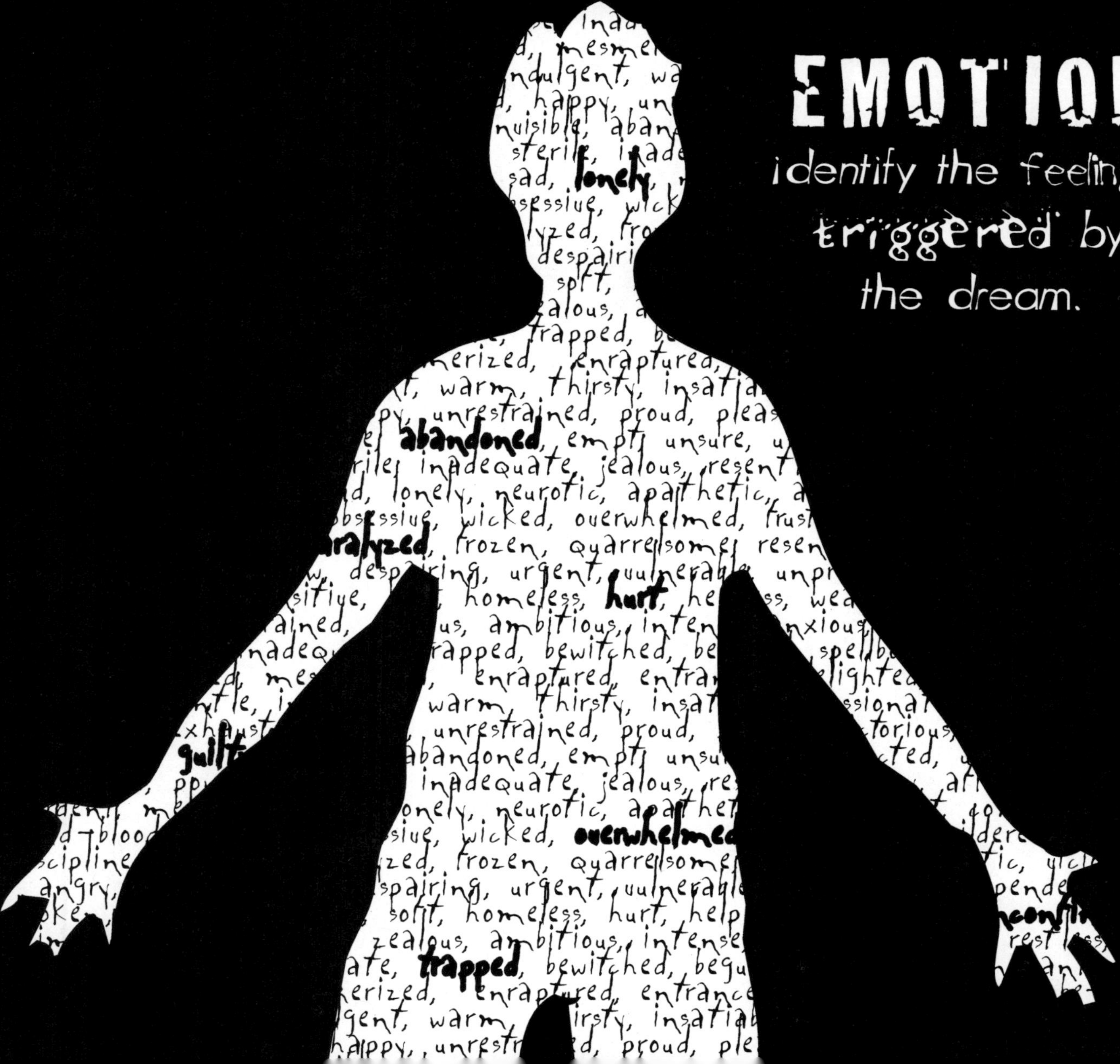

EMOTION

identify the feelings triggered by the dream.

IDIOSYNCRASY

Notice the most PECULIAR images and activities in the dream.

CONFLICT

Are there **opposing forces** in the dream?

CONFLICT

Are there
opposing forces
in the dream?

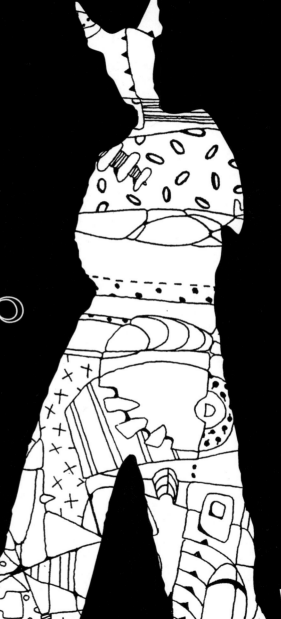

My snake is not your snake.

Freya Diamond

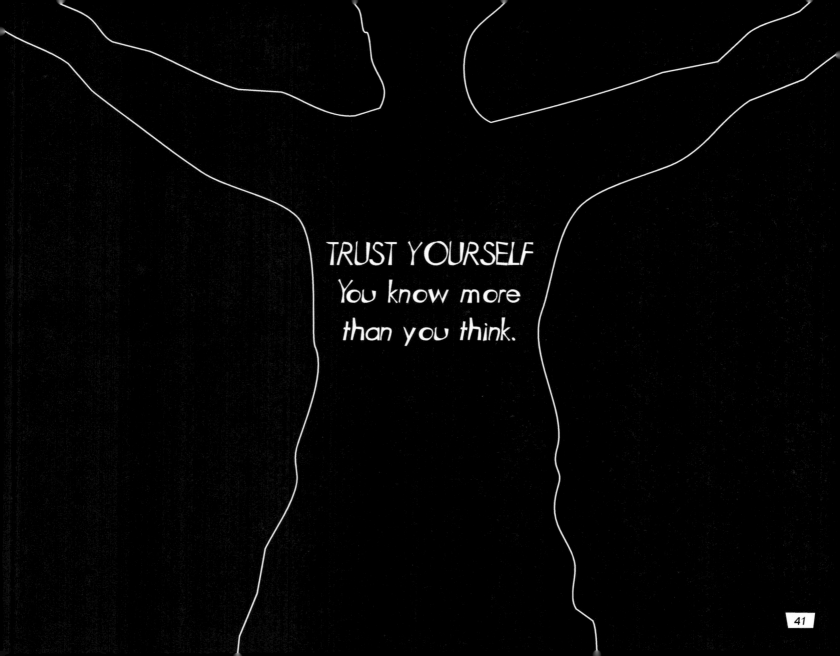

YOUR PERSONAL DREAM SYMBOL DICTIONARY

Write what you know about a DREAM IMAGE.

What details and facts can you crystallize?

What emotions are evoked?

What do you BELIEVE
and remember
about each image?

What connections can
you make with the
events and
feelings in waking life?

PEOPLE

Who are the PEOPLE in the dream?

What are they saying or doing?

Is there an antagonist or an ally?

How old are they?

Have you known any of them before?

What is their relationship

to your personal history and experience?

If people are UNFAMILIAR, how would you describe them?

What is YOUR role in the dream?

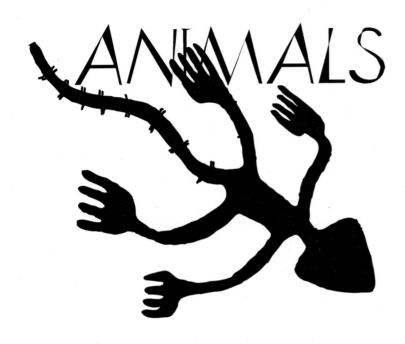

What kind of ANIMALS inhabit this dreamscape?

What PHYSICAL attributes do they possess?

How do they move
and interact with others?

How do you feel about

these CREATURES in walking life?

Do your dream ANIMALS
reflect an aspect of YOU?

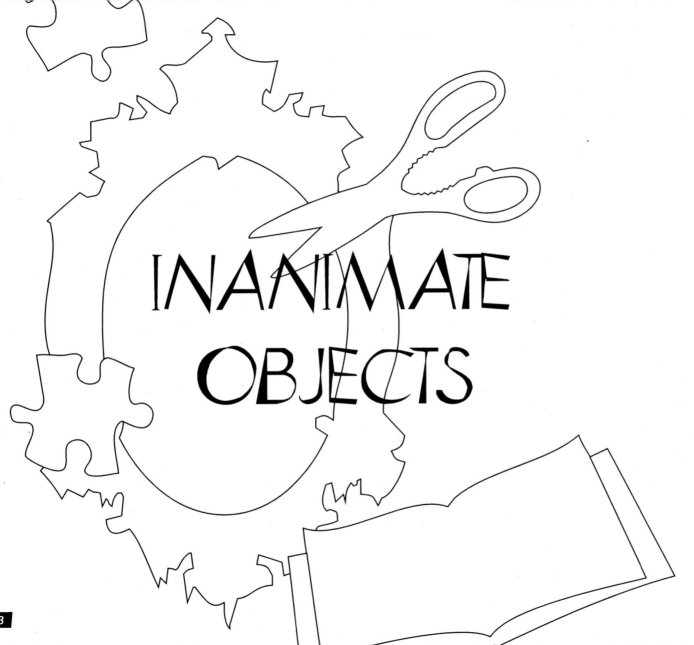

Can you describe
a DREAM OBJECT?

What is its
size, form and FUNCTION?

What is its
significance to you?

Where does this DREAM take place?

Is the setting
interior or exterior?

Is this environment
forbidding, foreboding or inviting?

EMOTIONS

insatiable, passionat
proud, please
abandoned
sterile
melancholy, sad
hostile
undisciplined
sarcastic, vicious
unprotected
hurt
weak, wild
anxious
unburden
savvy
ambival
overwhelm
enchanted
tender, benevolen
gluttonous, ecstatic
victorious, weightless
unsure, unprotected
jealous
affectio
lonely, neurotic
obsessive, wicked
frustrate
quarrelsome
vicious, angry
despairing, urgent
protected, dependen
crushed, sensitive, soft
impulsive, unrestrained

How does the dream
make you feel
upon WAKING?

What memories
do these feelings evoke?

WORDPLAY

Can you identify
the *puns*
and emotionally charged words
in your dream?

Look for words that have
several different meanings,
sounds or spellings.

Create definitions for
IDIOMS, jargon, and SLANG.

DREAM DICTIONARY

Keep your associations in a journal or computer file.

Add to it whenever you work on a DREAM.

Building your own lexicon will help you to *notice* recurring themes.

Be patient with all that is unsolved in your heart.
Try to love the Questions Themselves.
Do not now seek the answers
which cannot be given,
Because you would not be able to live them.
And the point is to live everything.
Live the question, now.
Perhaps you will then, gradually,
without noticing it,
live along some distant day into the answers.

Rainer Maria Rilke

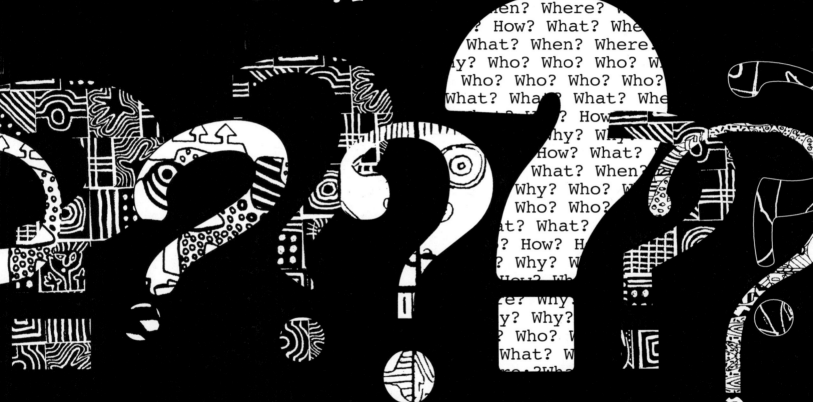

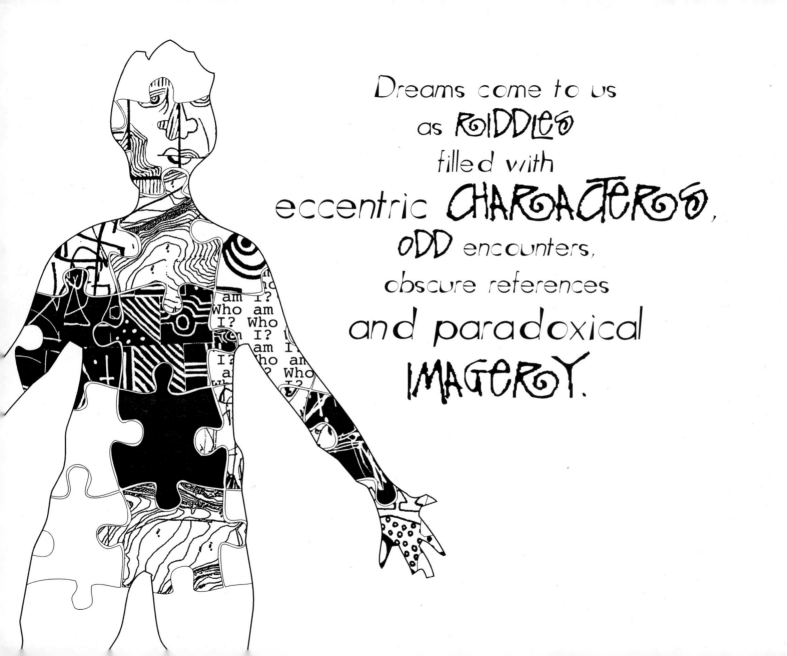

They haunt us with reverberations of the unknown and the unfathomable.

Dreams are MYSTERIOUS.

Can you allow yourself to live in the realm of uncertainty?

Where are the connections and disconnections?

What is **incongruous**, inconsistent, **irrational**?

What is uncomfortable? frustrating? **scary?**

Who is extraordinary, intriguing, peculiar?

Can you write pages of Questions without any need to find answers?

Can you question it all?

*The eye you see
is not an eye
because you see it;
It is an eye
because it sees you.*

Antonio Machado

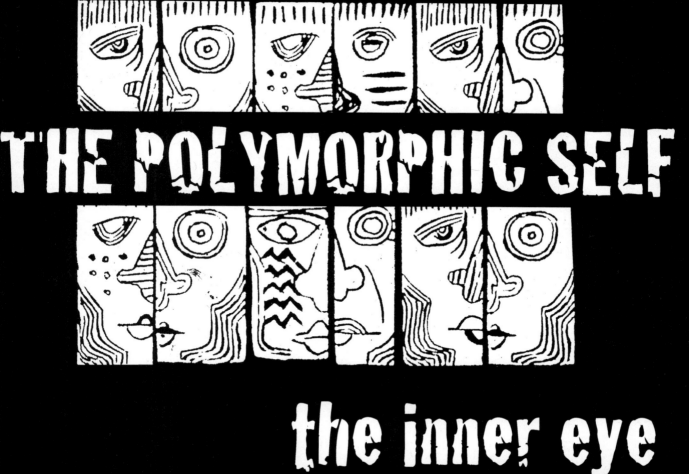

I AM THE CURVING PATH I AM THE ENTRANCE TO A SACRED CAVE I HAVE BEEN OPENED UP I AM ARTIFICIAL LIGHT I AM A RED FLOWER THAT GROWS IN A DARK CAVE I BLOOM IN THE DARK I AM HUGE AND POWERFUL I LIVE WITHIN SOLID ROCK I AM THE COLOR OF FIRE AND PASSION I AM THE WARRIOR I AM RED PULSING BLOOD I AM DARKNESS I AM INTIMIDATING I AM DANGER I BURN HOT I WILL ALWAYS FIND MY WAY BACK TO DEEP WATERS I AM A CARNIVAL RIDE I AM WHAT THRILLS ME I AM AN UNGRASPED HAND I AM HOLDING A WILD ANIMAL'S HEAD I AM FLAT I AM A DIRTY WINDOW I AM A PRECARIOUS EDGE I AM DISCOMFORT I AM A FEAR OF HEIGHTS I AM A CARNIVAL RIDE I AM THRILLING I AM EXCITING I AM SCARY I AM WHAT FRIGHTENS ME I AM UTTERLY SAFE AND SUPPORTED I HAVE NO HANDS I AM A BROKEN WASHING MACHINE I AM A DRIPPING SINK I AM AN OVERFLOWING BATHTUB I AM A CRACKED FOUNDATION I AM THE OLD CANDY WRAPPER UNDER THE COUCH I AM GLUTTONY I AM GLAMOUR I AM A SHADOW LURKING I AM DIRT I AM A COLLAPSING WALL I AM FREEDOM I AM A PRISONER I AM TORN NYLONS I AM POINTY TOED UNCOMFORTABLE SHOES I AM A HOT DOG WITH RELISH I HAVE LEGS AS LONG AS FLAGPOLES I AM A BOBCAT STUCK UP ON A POLE I AM THE ELEPHANT THAT DIED I AM DEAD I AM ALIVE AGAIN I AM A BURNED SCARRED BUFFALO I AM A THIEF I AM THE ONE WHO STALKS YOU I AM A HELPLESS VICTIM I AM AN OWL BORN OUT OF A STREETLAMP I AM A STRUGGLING MOTH I AM AFRAID OF MYSELF I AM LOST IN DARKNESS I HAVE FORGOTTEN WHO I AM I AM DRUNK I AM WORN OUT SOLES SOULS I AM A TRAIL OF POPPED BALLOONS I AM AN OLD WOMAN AND NO ONE LOVES ME I DON'T HAVE A VIEW I AM BLACK I AM BLUE I AM A ROOM THAT HAS A VIEW I AM A SLIDING GLASS DOOR TRANSPARENT I CAN BE SEEN THROUGH I AM NEUTRAL I AM MOVING SIDE TO SIDE I AM THE AMBIGUOUS I MAKE NO PUNCTUAL SENSE I AM YOUR FAMILIAR I AM INSIDE YOU I AM A SHORT HAIRED BLACK CAT I AM INVISIBLE I AM A BIRD I AM STANDING OUT HERE I AM THE BLUEBIRD I AM WOUNDED I AM THE ONLY MAN IN THE MOVIE THEATRE I AM SAD DEPRESSED MALE ENERGY I AM A MALE I NEED CLOSENESS AND CAMARADERIE I AM COMMUNITY I AM THE ANTIDOTE TO ISOLATION I AM LOVED AND CHERISHED BY SOME AND I AM THE CURVING PATH I AM THE ENTRANCE TO A SACRED CAVE I HAVE BEEN OPENED UP I AM ARTIFICIAL LIGHT I AM A RED FLOWER THAT GROWS IN A DARK CAVE I BLOOM IN THE DARK I AM HUGE AND POWERFUL I LIVE WITHIN SOLID ROCK I AM THE COLOR OF FIRE AND PASSION I AM THE WARRIOR I AM RED PULSING BLOOD I AM DARKNESS I AM INTIMIDATING I AM DANGER I BURN HOT I WILL ALWAYS FIND MY WAY BACK TO DEEP WATERS I AM A CARNIVAL RIDE I AM WHAT FRIGHTENS ME I AM AN UNGRASPED HAND I AM HOLDING A WILD ANIMAL'S HEAD I AM FLAT I AM A DIRTY WINDOW I AM A PRECARIOUS EDGE I AM DISCOMFORT I AM A FEAR OF HEIGHTS I AM A CARNIVAL RIDE I AM THRILLING I AM EXCITING I AM SCARY I AM WHAT FRIGHTENS ME I AM UTTERLY SAFE AND SUPPORTED I HAVE NO HANDS I AM A BROKEN WASHING MACHINE I AM A DRIPPING SINK I AM AN OVERFLOWING

Every night,
in our dreams,

we CREATE
a multitude of images
that reflect

the many aspects of ourselves,

our attitudes, our characteristics,

our relationships to OTHERS.

Each CHARACTER, ANIMAL or vehicle is a **reflection** of our eccentricities, peculiarities, behavior, and temperament.

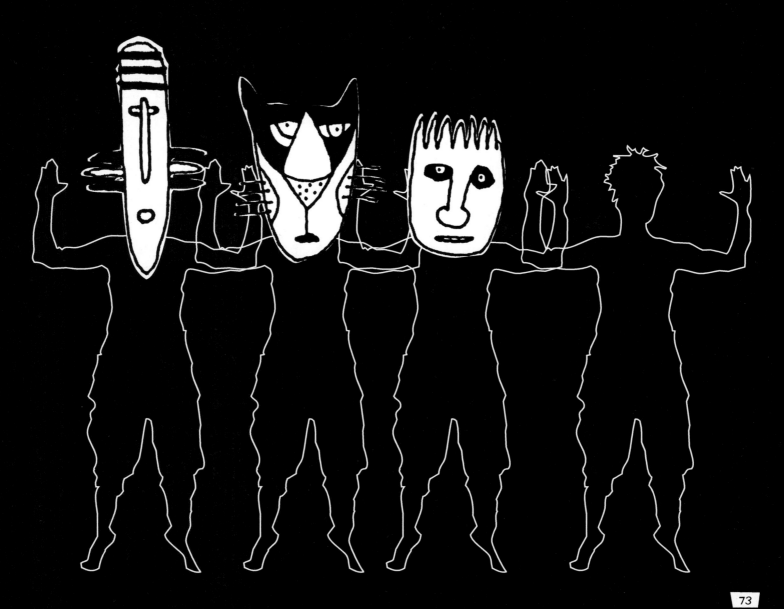

Even the inanimate objects
embody aspects of our identities...
the *good*, the **bad**, and the ugly.

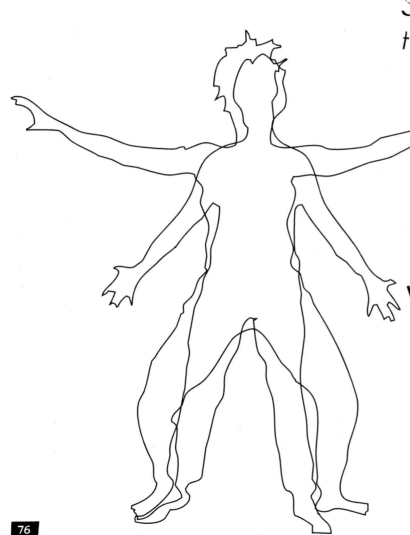

Shift your point of view to take on the identities of each of your dream images.

Let go of who you think you are.

Become empty of intention or ego.

Write a list

Begin each line with

I am...

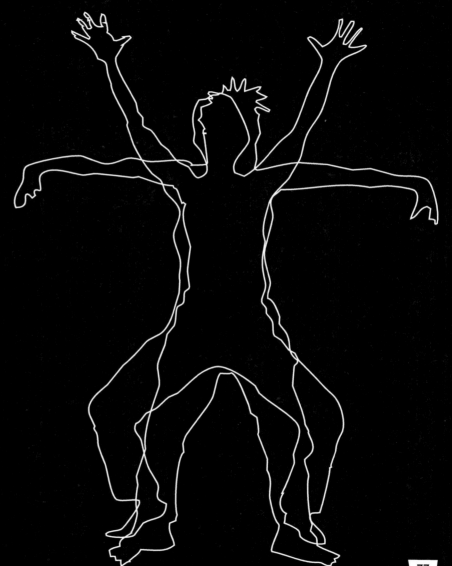

dark cave | bloom in the dark | am huge and powerful | live within solid rock | am the color of fire and passion | am the
am red pulsing blood | am darkness | am intimidating | am danger | burn hot | will always find my way back to deep w
n a carnival ride | am what frightens me | am an ungrasped hand | am holding a wild animals head | am flat | am a dirty wi
n a precarious edge | am discomfort | a fear of heights | am a c nival ride | am thrilling | am exciting | am scary
t frightens me | am utterly safe and suppo have no hands or fe am a broken washing machine | am a dripping s
an overflowing bathtub | am a walrus | am cracked foundation | an e old candy wrapper under the couch | am glutto
a broken window | am a shadow lurking | am dirt | am a collapsing wa | am freedom | am my mothers dress | am torn n
n pointy toed uncomfortable shoes | am a ho dog with relish | am a orse with legs as long as flagpoles | am a bobcat
on a pole | am the elephant that needs rescui | am am a again | am a burned scarred buffalo | am a thief
predator that stalks you | am a helpless victim m a ou a streetlamp | am a struggle | am doubt | am afra
elf | am lost in darkness | have forgotten who am nk shoes without soles souls | am a trail of popped ba
n an old woman and no one loves me | am a r vie am black | am blue am a room that has a view
g glass door | am transp rent | can be seen th gh e am moving side to e am the ambiguity | am you
tual sense | am your fam am inside you a ck cat | am not ack am blue | am a bird | am sta
here | am the bluebird | am w am mottle am the m e movie theatre | am sad depressed
gy | am a consoling spirit | am a c community | am the antidote to a sense of
| am memory | am cherished by some an e entrance to a sacred cave | have been opene
n artificial light | am a red flower that grows in a in the dark | am huge and powerful | live within solid
n the color of fire and passion | am the warrior od | am darkness | am intimidating | am danger | burr
ll always find my way back to deep waters | a what frightens me | am an ungrasped hand | am ho
ld animals head | am flat | am a dirty windo am e am discomfort | am a fear of heights | am a ca
am thrilling | am exciting | am scary a what f am rly safe and supported | have no hands or feet
oken washing machine | am a dripping si | am a bathtub am a walrus | am a cracked foundation | am the
y wrapper under the couch | am glu | am a am a adow lurking | am dirt | am a collapsing wall
edom | am my mothers dress | am n nylons ncomfor e shoes | am a hot dog with relish | am a h
legs as long as flagpoles | am a bobcat stuck u e elep that needs rescuing | am dead | am alive
n a burned scarred buffalo | am a thief | am ts you | am a helpless victim | am an owl born out
etlamp | am a struggle | am doubt | am afra darkness | have forgotten who am | am drunk
es without soles souls | am a trail of poppe am an and no one loves me | am a room | have a vie
black | am blue | am a room that has a vie sliding am transparent | can be seen through | am neu
moving side to side | am the ambiguity a tinctual our familiar | am inside you | am a short haired
am not black | am blue | am a bird ar ut here in ebird am wounded | am mottled | am so sad
man in the movie theatre | am sad depre energy a g spirit | am a clown | am closeness and camar
| am community | am the antidote to a se ation am hor m cherished by some and | am the curving path
entrance to a sacred cave | have been o am arti ph m a red flower that grows in a dark cave | bloo
dark | am huge and powerful | live within s k am the e and passion | am the warrior | am red pulsing b
n darkness | am intimidating | am danger ot | will alw y way back to deep waters | am a carnival ride
t frightens me | am an ungrasped hand a ding a wild ani am flat | am a dirty window | am a precarious
n discomfort | am a fear of heights a rnival ride | am exciting | am scary | am what frightens me
ly safe and supported | have no hands eet | am a broken w hing machine | am a dripping sink | am an overflowing
| am a walrus | am a cracked foundation am the old candy wrap er under the couch | am gluttony | am a broken wind
a shadow lurking | am dirt | am a collapsing wall | am freedom | am my mothers dress | am torn nylons | am pointy

BECOME ONE WITH YOUR DREAM

SO THAT THE HEART OF EACH CHARACTER
BEATS IN YOUR OWN HEART

all *landscapes* are your own body

all actions and ACTIVITIES are happening to you

all feelings are your own

all inanimate **objects** are aspects of you

all emotions flow through your veins

Elaborate on what you see, sense and how you feel.

*If you don't know
where you're going,
every road
will lead you there.*

CARTOGRAPHER

mapping the dreamscape

A dream is a personal atlas
of where we are in our lives,
where we have come from
and where we are going.

The dream takes us on a voyage
   beneath the surface of what is known
      and elevates us to peaks of what is possible.

TERRA INCOGNITA

Traversing the hemispheres of the night mind can be a daunting journey if we have no way to find our bearings.

We may awaken **feeling lost** and disoriented **with no way** to ground our experience in this sea of **SHIFTING TIDES.**

CREATE AN OVERVIEW OF YOUR DREAM.

Use symbols, codes, arrows, and overlap spheres of influence. Make connections. Record movements and patterns of migration. Chart the turnarounds, escape routes,

Diagram the TWISTS AND TURNS. Create bridges. Indicate the crossroads. Mark the boundaries, the edges, the obstacles, the dead ends, short cuts, detours, alternate routes.

Leap and the net will appear.

John Burroughs

SYNCHRONICITY

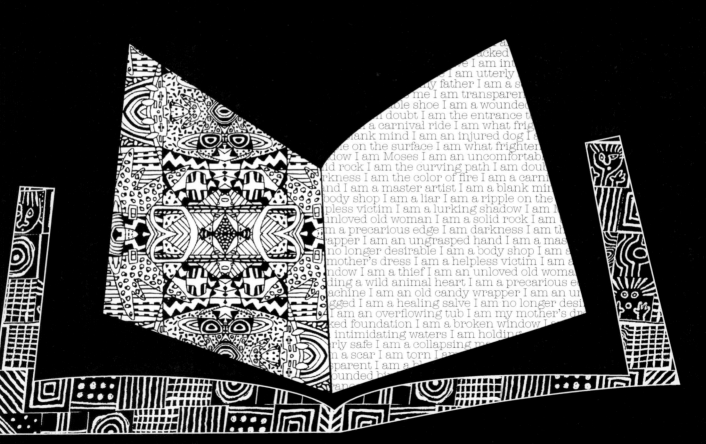

SYNCHRONICITY
is a pattern of unrelated chances
which are often interpreted as

meaningful coincidences.

It is that rare occurrence
when a set of unconnected events
have the serendipitous quality of coming together
in the right time and the right place.

Synchronicity inspires a sense of wonder and awe
at the providential nature of our experience.

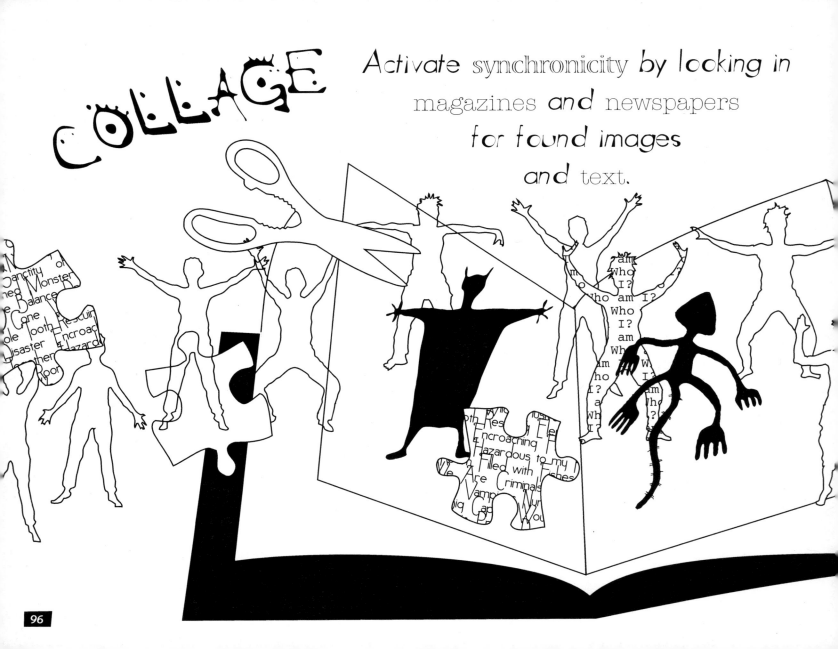

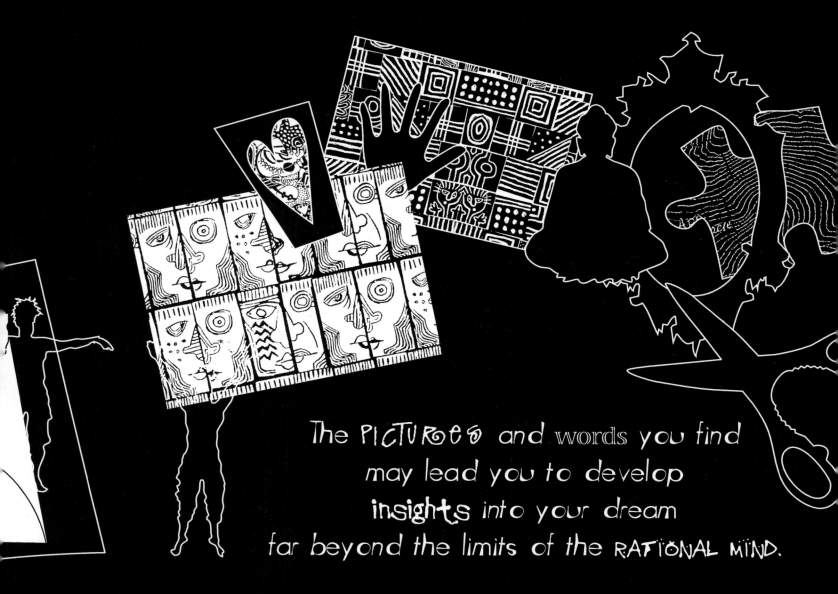

Let go of your preconceived idea of the MEANING of your dream.

Throw yourself at the mercy of the process of hunting and gathering.

For your collage, collect photographs and text that fascinate, Disturb or intrigue you.

Choose IMAGES that represent the emotional content of your dream.

SERENDIPITY

Allow INSTINCT
and stream of consciousness
to guide you beyond
the threshold of
normal perception.

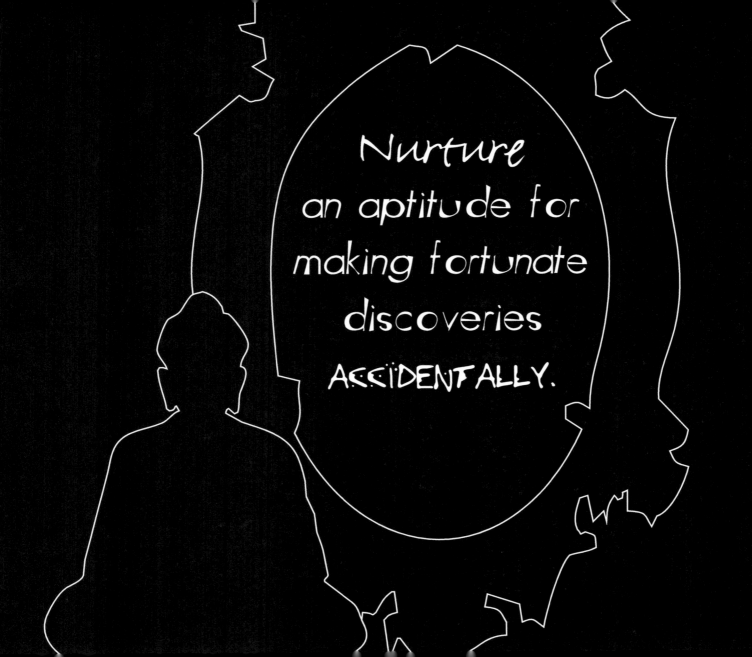

Meddle with your notion of the dream.

Allow **found images** to play their TRICKS.

Let your dream images SHIFT shapes.

Let go of the INTERFERENCE of your mind.
Surrender yourself to what you find.

Open yourself to what finds you.

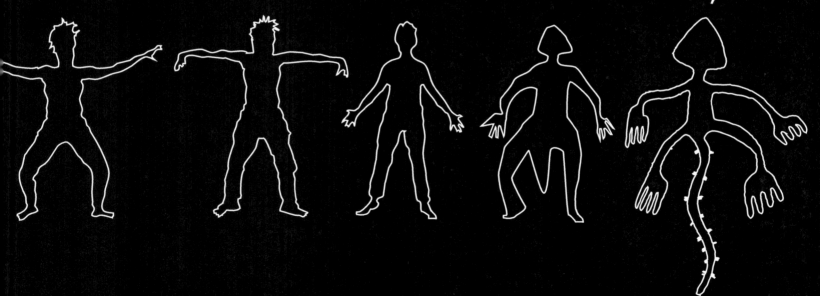

When the heart weeps
for what is lost,
the soul rejoices
for what it has found

Amy Zemer and
Monte Farber

POUR YOUR HEART OUT

Our dreams are the repository
of our deepest *feelings*.

They call to us
from the innermost
center
of our beings.

They touch us in our tenderest places with the depth of our longing, our **sorrows** and our joys.

Dreams ENCHANT us

with euphoria,

they arouse our

passions,

they taunt us with jealousy,

they envelop us

in heartbreak,

they fill us with wonder

and mystery.

From the depths of your dream,
allow your heart to **burst open**
and overflow into your journal.

Fill your pages with
scribbled words
and
spilled ink.

Let your words
RUSH OUT
without regard
for punctuat!on or grammar.

Permit words to
tumble & flow
without judgment.

Give voice to your grief, your **sorrow**, your *longing*.

Let your imagination surrender to

vulnerability, desire, compassion.

Abandon yourself

to all that has been

locked inside.

One does not become enlightened
by imagining figures of light,
but by making the darkness conscious

Carl Gustav Jung

It takes **courage**
to record and acknowledge
the **dark** emotional content
of dreams.

Often we are confronted with
crazy, complex narratives which can be
confusing, disturbing, or
frightening.

Scenes of forbidden love, regrets, obsessions, cravings may surge up from our depths;

feelings of being trapped, manipulated or frustrated may bruise us with despair.

Sift through the **debris**, the ashes, and the e c h o e s of the dark corners of your dream for a shadow image.

In the privacy of your journal become a **bogey man**, a p h a n t o m , a **spook**.

Reveal the dark undercurrents in your dream.

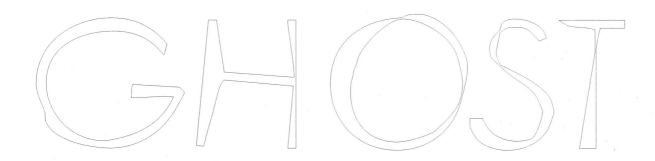

Express all of your pent up feelings.

Speak in a whisper with the voice of an apparition.

WRITING

sing softly and sigh

Whimper and weep

Moan and lament

Let the wind of your voice blow through the cracks of your inner mysteries.

Pry **open your** closely guarded secrets.

Give **voice** to all that has been lying **dormant**.

When you have finished your **ghost writing,**

create a ceremony
to insure that all of your secrets will be safe.

burn, crush, tear, shred your writing. Ceremonially burn, crush, tear, burn, crush, tear, shred your writing. Cereme burn, crush, tear, shred

Ceremonially burn, crush, tear, shred your writing. Ceremonially burn, crush, tear, shred your writing. Ceremonially burn, crush, tear, shred your writing. Ceremonially burn, crush, te

A dream unexplored
is like a letter unopened

Talmud

Dreams frequently present VIVID IMAGES filled with wonder and permeated with mystery.

We wake up haunted by a **fragment** of

a vision,

a *taste*,

a touch,

an encounter.

We remain
captivated
by a sensation,
a phrase,
a **Loss** or
a *love.*

The narrative of the dream may seem **incomplete** or the ending may be

interrupted;

yet we **awaken** with a state of heightened emotion.

wonder pleasure peace foolishness regret sweetness arrogance bitterness warmth tenderness wonder pleasure peace foolishness regret sweetness arrogance disappointment sacrifice warmth tenderness wonder pleasure peace foolishness loneliness separation disappointment sacrifice warmth tenderness wonder sacredness loneliness separation disappointment sacrifice warmth bitterness sacredness loneliness separation disappointment sacrifice arrogance bitterness sacredness loneliness separation disappointment sweetness arrogance bitterness sacredness loneliness separation regret sweetness arrogance bitterness sacredness loneliness foolishness regret sweetness arrogance bitterness sacredness peace foolishness regret sweetness arrogance bitterness pleasure peace foolishness regret sweetness wonder pleasure peace foolishness regret tenderness wonder pleasure peace foolishness warmth tenderness wonder pleasure sacrifice warmth tenderness wonder disappointment sacrifice warmth separation disappointment sacrifice loneliness separation disappointment sacredness loneliness separation *bitterness sacredness loneliness separation disappointment sacrifice warmth tenderness wonder pleasure peace foolishness regret sweetness arrogance* (repeating)

Write in a stream of unending sentences

without taking the pen off the page.

Turn off your internal editor.

Become empty of intention or ego.

Let the image speak. Let the image **speak**. Let the image **speak**.

Allow thoughts to tumble out unstructured, raw and chaotic.

Fill your letter with memories evoked by the dream.

Invite your dream image to remember **moments** of warmth, tenderness, pleasure or peace.

Allow your image to disclose reveries of loneliness, separation, disappointment or sacrifice.

Listen to the image confiding secrets of foolishness, arrogance or **regret.**

Let the image invoke the sweet, the bitter, the **painful**, the sacred.

Allow your dream image to reveal all that has been unspoken

Forget safety.
Live where you fear to live.
Destroy your reputation.
Be notorious.

Rumi

THE POISON PEN

confronting the inner bully

Dreams are filled with precarious, CHAOTIC and **perplexing bullies** and **tyrants.**

They can **cut** right through to our souls

in an instant.

They **TAUNT** us
they reproach us,
they mock us.

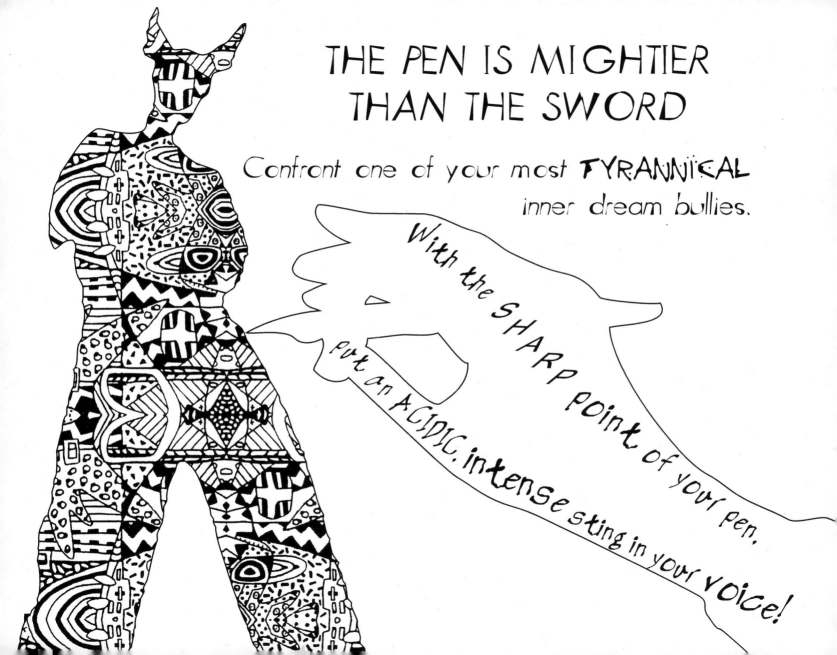

Strike
with your most poisonous,
accusatory, irritated barbs
at your edgiest dream images.

Defend yourself
with a sharp,
THREATENING
bitter tone of voice!

Write the words you've always wanted to write. Confront your villains! Conquer impossible odds! Triumph over **CONFLICT!** Escape from the inescapable!

Rant and Rave with annoyance or tension!

Be insulting, maddening, Crazy, Rude!

Let your feelings toward your inner bully

explode

onto the page!

Ask questions.
Demand responses.

Go ballistic!

Be brave, be annoying, be curious,
be insane, be fearless!

When we dream,
we can learn to bring back something of value to society.
The creative dreamer does not return empty-handed.
He or she is an explorer of the dream world,
returning with a song, a dance, a cure,
with information about the future,
information about a distant place
or a new idea of some kind.

David Coxhead and Susan Hiller

A dream is a museum of memories,

ANCESTRAL connections, recollections, and reminiscences;

it is **filled** with **fragile** relics, peculiar old stuff;

things REMEMBERED and things forgotten.

HONOR YOUR DREAM

Find ways

to show *reverence*

towards your dreams

by collecting

memorabilia,

souvenirs,

and

ephemera

of dream images.

TREASURE HUNT

Be on the lookout for mementos, antiquities, curiosities, icons, artifacts with attributes that recall **fragments** of your dreams.

Search for keepsakes that resonate with the CHARACTERS, ANIMALS, objects, colors and **emotions** of your dream.

CREATE A DREAM ALTAR

Display Groupings of found **fragments** and artifacts.

handiwork reminder keepsake ancestral connection odds and ends ephemera past life object of reverence mummy ghost memories shrine icon stones relic curiosities artifact memorabilia souvenir trophy historical sentimental object custom belief lost civilization treasure trove article handiwork reminder keepsake ancestral connection odds and ends ephemera past life object of reverence mummy ghost memories shrine icon stones relic curiosities artifact memorabilia souvenir trophy historical sentimental object custom belief lost civilization treasure trove article handiwork reminder keepsake ancestral connection odds and ends ephemera past life object of reverence mummy ghost memories shrine icon stones relic curiosities artifact memorabilia souvenir trophy historical sentimental object custom belief lost civilization treasure trove article handiwork reminder keepsake ancestral connection odds and ends ephemera shrine icon trophy h

Wrap your written memories and musings together into sacred bundles. Keep the spirits in your dreams ALIVE.

What the caterpillar calls
the end of the world,
the master calls
a butterfly.

Richard Bach

There is a transcendent voice
that calls
from the **depths** of the dream.

It takes time
to hear
what it
has to say.

Sometimes dreams wake us with a sense of balance, purity, simplicity, an effortless moment of charm or beauty.

surrender to the sublime.

Welcome these precious, unexpected experiences.

Find a quiet place
to sit in stillness.

Re-enter the dream.

Center yourself
with eyes closed
for a few moments.

Soak up the
inexplicable
presence
within the dream.

Hold the dream in your imagination, open it.
Allow the images to move without guidance.
When we experience the grace in the dream,
Commune with the mystery.

turn it around, move inside it.

without direction, without restriction, without destination.

a sense of illumination washes over us.

Let it be.

THE DREAM TEAM

Sean Wells | Freya Diamond | Alex Fischer | Jean Stratton

This book, forged in friendship, mutual respect and admiration, exists as the manifestation of a work of love between four follow dreamers who have accompanied me for years in the Art of the Dream workshops. Sean, Freya, Alex and Jean are bright, articulate, and creative women who share my graphic aesthetic as well as my commitment to excellence. As a team, we are focused, efficient and just a bit wildish. Together we have shared the breathtaking insight of deep inner work coupled with just the right seasoning of joy and whimsy. The raw material from years of experiential workshops has been sifted and simmered; honed and sharpened; reworked and refined.

This extraordinary troupe has spun my straw into gold.

VICTORIA RABINOWE

Victoria is an artist, an educator and a DreamTender. Dreams provide the substance, spirit and depth of her paintings, drawings, digital art and hand-bound books. Her artwork has been exhibited in museums, galleries and universities throughout the United States and Japan including The Legion of Honor of The Fine Arts Museum of San Francisco, The Craft and Folk Art Museum in Los Angeles, and the Kyoto College of Arts & Crafts.

Since 1991, Victoria has developed a unique body of guided techniques in dream work, image making and creative writing. She has taught over five hundred workshops, seminars and retreats in the *Art of the Dream* for therapists, educators, spiritual guidance counselors, writers and artists. She is certified in Advanced DreamTending through Pacifica Graduate Institute, and she is an annual presenter at the International Association for the Study of Dreams.

As the chairperson and program director for the Santa Fe Book Arts Group (B.A.G.) from 1993-2005, she initiated educational programs, museum and gallery exhibitions for 250 Santa Fe artists interested in the inventive spirit of the book form as a vessel for creative expression. As the founder and former co-owner of the Santa Fe Weaving Gallery from 1975-1991, she was a pioneer in the field of Wearable Arts in America in the latter twentieth century.

DREAM

THE BLIND BOATMAN

The waves are high.
A boat comes to pick me up.
It is an odd little boat.
I am excited but concerned.
The little boat will get tossed around
on these huge waves.
Will I be able to handle it?

An old man with a cane shuffles ashore
to get me.
He can barely see or walk.
He is the captain of the boat.

SEAN WELLS

Sean has been mentored by Victoria as an artist, businesswoman and dreamer since 1984. As Victoria's Little Sister in the Big Brothers Big Sisters Program, Sean has been introduced to fiber arts, ceramics, silk painting, spinning, weaving, dyeing, site sketching, watercolor, print making, book arts as well as exposure to the business side of art with training at the Santa Fe Weaving Gallery.

Sean has reciprocated by assisting Victoria's study of digital media with training in photoshop and web design. She has designed Victoria's website.

Graduating with a BS in Architecture from the University of Virginia, Sean maintains a strong relationship with the arts participating in public art projects. She co-founded Twilight Design Studio with her husband where they have been designing award winning architectural works and graphics since 1997.

DREAM

SINKING FEELING

I allow the car to fly off
to the green, murky waters below.

As we fly, I take a deep breath.

I see everyone struggling
to get out of the car
to get to the surface,
but I know it is best to wait.

The car sinks and I begin to pull myself out.

I look up and can see the others
swimming to the surface.

I am not scared.
I am struck by the beauty of the sight.
I must act.

FREYA DIAMOND

Freya Diamond is Victoria's teaching assistant. She has been attending the *Art of the Dream* workshops since their inception in 1993. She has completed over 450 creative dream explorations consisting of mandalas, game boards, altars, maps, divination cards and scrolls. She has transformed over 300 of these dream projects into one-of-a-kind books featuring concertinas, three layer carousels, origami folds, pop-up books, flag books, coptic books and tunnel books.

Freya began actively remembering and recording her dreams over 25 years ago, when she was dealing with serious illnesses. She found both healing and consolation within her night time narratives. A book artist, with a background in design and fine arts, Freya has shown her work in exhibitions across the country.

DREAM

THE STAMP SIGN

I feel it is time to leave this place.
I stamp my new serpent stamp
black on the floor
to give a sign of the leaving.

Others disagree with me
and stamp over it in beautiful pastels
to camouflage the ones I have made.

However,
I know what is under it all.

ALEX FISCHER

Alex Fischer is a faithful participant in the Art of the Dream workshops and believes strongly in the power of dreams to guide and shape our lives. She has been recording her dreams since she was small, first using scribbles and then actual words once she learned how to write.

Alex is a mixed media artist whose love of bookmaking has evolved into her serving a term as President of the Santa Fe Book Arts Group. She has shown her work in galleries in California and New Mexico for several years. Alex has offered workshops in memoir and collage for mothers and daughters to share their stories together.

A retired Registered Nurse, Alex worked many years in the mental health field as case manager for the homeless mentally ill and with families-at-risk. She co-founded a nonprofit organization that provided education, prevention and intervention in school programs as well as the larger community, dedicated to breaking the cycle of domestic violence. While serving on the first child abuse prevention council in Inyo County, California, she worked to increase interagency communication to improve client care. She has used the creative arts with those affected by family violence or sexual assault to assist them in expressing feelings that might otherwise be difficult to communicate.

DREAM

CARRYING THE BISHOP

I live in an outdoor convent.
Today I am to carry a Bishop up the mountain.
It is a test.
Somehow his body
has been laced into my shoe.
He has become very small.
I start up the mountain.

Now he is full-sized.
He is in my large backpack.
I wonder why I am being asked
to do this.
How can I possibly bear his weight?

JEAN STRATTON

Jean Stratton has been interested in dream work since the 1970s when she attended workshops on dream work and Jungian psychology at the Pecos Benedictine Monastery in New Mexico. Synchronistically with her partial retirement as an educator, she found the *Art of the Dream* group and has been involved in the weekly workshop at Victoria's studio since 2001.

Jean has worked as a high school journalism, yearbook and humanities teacher and most recently as senior consultant and statewide director of Re:Learning New Mexico, a state supported systemic reform program for education. Jean has presented hundreds of workshops for teachers across the state of New Mexico, most recently specializing in Writing across the Curriculum and Active Literacy. She has incorporated many of the techniques of collage and bookmaking she learned in the *Art of the Dream* workshops in her teacher training presentations.

DREAM

KINDERGARTEN BOOKS

I am a kindergarten teacher
It is the first day of school.
I am in the classroom.
I have beautiful suede covered books
for each child.
Each book is decorated with gemlike stones.
Inside each book are stories
from exotic countries.

Pages are cut in the middle to make little pockets.
Each pocket holds tiny boxes
shaped like hearts, crescents, pyramids,
all beautifully decorated.

Each child is to put three things into her box —
a wish,
a mantra
and a secret word.

SUSAN HILL
(FOREWORD)

For more than a decade, Susan Hill has engaged in the study of dreams, understanding the links between Dreams and Imagination, Dreams and a Collective World Story. She has taught creative workshops on Dream, traveled to study dreams in magical places and, like Victoria, is certified by Pacifica Graduate Institute for studies in Advanced DreamTending.

Susan is an accomplished visual artist and community arts director living in Venice, California. Since 1975, she has worked primarily in multi-disciplinary collaborative arts programs and projects among marginalized constituencies to create public work, understanding, and peaceful social change.

Mentored by Judy Chicago, the innovative activist feminist artist, and Judy Baca, an extraordinary muralist, activist, and educator, Susan has created teaching opportunities, theatre companies, community arts programs and conferences engaging a diversified network of professional artists in paid, visible, socially responsible endeavors.

DREAM

SILVER SPIRALS

I am walking barefoot on a long, sandy road.
I can see the road stretch to the horizon.
Just ahead,
very low,
nearly touching me,
is a huge soft brown cloud
laced with sparkling silver spirals.

ETHICS STATEMENT

Although working with dreams creatively may feel therapeutic, the projects included in this book are not intended to be therapy. Dream work outside a clinical setting is not a substitute for psychotherapy or other professional treatment.

This book reflects the statement of ethics of the International Association for the Study of Dreams which follows:

We support an approach to dream work and dream sharing that respects the dreamer's dignity and integrity, and which recognizes the dreamer as the decision-maker regarding the significance of the dream. Systems of dream work that assign authority or knowledge of the dream's meanings to someone other than the dreamer can be misleading, incorrect, or harmful.

Ethical dream work helps the dreamer work with his/her own dream images, feelings, and associations, and guides the dreamer to more fully experience, appreciate and understand the dream.

Every dream may have multiple meanings, and different techniques may be reasonably employed to touch these multiple layers of significance.

All dreams come in the service of healing and wholeness.

There are many excellent books available on dreaming. It is not within the scope of this book to cover the basic materials for the study of dreams.

The purpose of this book is to offer direct, simple techniques to help you explore your dreams with a minimum of research and reading.

For a bibliography, there is an excellent list of books about dreams recommended by

The International Association for the Study of Dreams | www.asdreams.org

Victoria Rabinowe welcomes email inquiries regarding dream workshops and dream group facilitator trainings.

To be placed on the mailing list to receive illustrated monthly calendars and advance notice of future publications, please contact VictoriaDreams@mac.com

Bright Shadow Press | Santa Fe, NM | VictoriaDreams@mac.com | www.VictoriaDreams.com